SOMETHING
THAT BELONGS TO YOU

Roald Hoffmann

for Fred and Lib
with affection

Roald
2015

DOS MADRES

2015

DOS MADRES PRESS INC.
P.O.Box 294, Loveland, Ohio 45140
www.dosmadres.com   editor@dosmadres.com

Dos Madres is dedicated to the belief that the small press is essential to the vitality of contemporary literature as a carrier of the new voice, as well as the older, sometimes forgotten voices of the past. And in an ever more virtual world, to the creation of fine books pleasing to the eye and hand.

Dos Madres is named in honor of Vera Murphy and Libbie Hughes, the "Dos Madres" whose contributions have made this press possible.

Dos Madres Press, Inc. is an Ohio Not For Profit Corporation and a 501 (c) (3) qualified public charity. Contributions are tax deductible.

Executive Editor: Robert J. Murphy

Illustration & Book Design: Elizabeth H. Murphy
www.illusionstudios.net

Typset in Adobe Garamond Pro
ISBN 978-1-939929-31-0
Library of Congress Control Number: 2015940954

First Edition

DEDICATED TO MY MOTHER AND FATHER

SOMETHING THAT BELONGS TO YOU

CAST

1992, Philadelphia
    Frieda Pressner, age 81
    Emile Pressner, 55, a physician, Frieda's son,
       with whose family Frieda lives
    Tamar Meiblum, 49, psychologist, Emile's wife
    Heather Pressner, 17, their daughter
    Danny Pressner, 13, their son
    Alla Olesko, 55, from Ukraine, Myroslav Olesko's
       daughter

1943, Gribniv, Ukraine, then German-occupied Poland,
now western Ukraine. Gribniv is a small village 20 miles
from the town Strody, in which the Pressner family lived
before WW II.
    Frieda Pressner, 32
       (played by older Frieda, or another actor)
    Emile Pressner, 6
       (played by Danny Pressner, or another actor)
    Myroslav Olesko, 48, Ukrainian school teacher
       in whose house the Pressners and Ernest
       Brandes (uncle Ernie, Frieda's brother) are hidden.
       Olesko is a nonspeaking role, in one scene only.
       Ernie is not in play, nor is Frieda's husband,
       Daniel, killed in 1943.

The play moves back and forth between Philadelphia and Gribniv. The Philadelphia setting is the interior of a small house in, say, the Mt. Airy area of Philadelphia. Much of the action takes place in a large kitchen, and in Frieda Pressner's room. The Gribniv setting is an attic, dimly lit. The attic in Ukraine with the rooms in Philadelphia may be combined in one set. Near the end of the play there is increasing "cross-over," 1992 characters appearing in the attic. At the end the two settings merge.

The action takes place over three months in 1992 in Philadelphia, and over a year, 1943, in Gribniv. The time sequence in 1943 is not important. The scenes opening the acts are in an otherworldly place, perhaps heaven.

Throughout play, the slash / marks a place where dialogue is interrupted by next line.

ACT 1

SCENE 1

Somewhere in heaven. Signs on scene say Heaven in Polish (niebo), Ukrainian (nebo), Hebrew (shamaim), English. God and angels, all played by characters in play. God looks like Groucho Marx, cigar and all. Or Mae West. His robe is whiter, more starched, than that of the angels. Some of them look pretty run down or spaced out. The angels wear placards (or have roughly printed on the back of their gowns, so as to identify them): Truth, Peace, Justice, Love. Everything is played as broadly as possible.

[Discordant noise. Cross talk by angels. Clash of cymbals.]

GOD: OK, OK, pipe down angels. This is not a Grateful Dead concert.

ANGEL 1: God, would you like to hear a joke? A blue angel joke?

GOD: Sure.

ANGEL 1: So a blue angel is eating the head of a fish, a carp. A red angel looks on, enviously. Finally he says: "I heard you blue angels are real smart. How come?" The blue angel says. "It's because we eat the heads of fish, of course. I have another one *(he pulls one out wrapped in a newspaper)* I'll sell it to you for 18 kopeks, my red friend." The red angel shells out the 18 kopeks, gets the head of another carp, eats it. At that moment a fish-monger comes by with a sign "Whole carp 5 kopeks." The red angel is furious, attacks the blue angel: "You sold me the head of a carp for 18 kopeks. But I can get the whole fish for 5!" The blue angel says "See, you're smarter already."

1

OTHER ANGELS: Boo… Love it!... Funny, it isn't… Tell me, is that a Jewish joke?

GOD: Stop it, stop it! *(Slowly.)* We are here for an experiment in *(Emphasis.)* democracy.

OTHER ANGELS: *(Not all together.)* We are with you, God baby….Right on, God….Listen to the man.

ANGEL 1: We are unanimously in favor of democracy *(Cheers all around.)*

GOD: The question before us is… *(He hems and haws, not being able to remember.)* What is the question before us?

ANGEL 1: Should we create Man? That's with a capital M, God. I mean, should you create Man, you're the one into the whole creator biz.

GOD: Yes, Most certainly. *(Loudly.)* Should we create Man? *(Aside to audience.)* It's a good idea to try out democracy on an unimportant issue. I mean… we could have talked about poppies. *(Beat.)* The plant, *(Beat.)* with the seeds, you know. *(Loud again, pompous.)* Yes. Man. And Woman. Let us hear the opinions of the four Attributes.

LOVE = ANGEL 2: *(Showing her/his placard, so there's no doubt who she is.)* I say Yes, let them be created. For they will dispense acts of love.

OTHER ANGELS: *(Not in unison.)* Notice she didn't say "he"? …Whooo, blondie's soft as always…. Love, shmove.

GOD: OK, OK. Back to work. *(He motions to Truth.)*

TRUTH = ANGEL 1: *(Pointing grandiosely to his/her placard.)* Truth votes No. For man is a bag of lies. Her too. They make up stories, at the slightest provocation. Anything they can get away with, they'll try.

OTHER ANGELS: *(Not together.)* So, who's real?... He's a good one to talk... Not everyone can afford diamonds...

GOD: Quiet, minions. Let's show some collegial respect.

ANGEL 1: An objection, God.

GOD: Yes, my child.

ANGEL 1: Sir, with all due respect. Love, Truth, Beauty...This is neoplatonic crap. Whoops *(Covers his mouth.)* That just came out. *(God nods it's OK.)* In the old country we didn't have "love," "truth," "peace." If you don't restore the purity /of the religion,...

GOD: *(Interrupts.)* Shut up. We have to be modern. Go on... *(He motions with his cigar to remaining "Attributes")* I like you guys, you're brief, not like those lawyers.

JUSTICE = ANGEL 3: Justice, I, say: Yes, let him be created, because he will do righteous deeds.

OTHER ANGELS: *(Not in unison.)* Yeah, we're for the righteous... But do we need them for this, isn't that our job?.... Good deeds, fat chance....

PEACE = ANGEL 4: Very simply: No, he is one mass of contention. He will make war. He will slaughter.

OTHER ANGELS: *(Not together.)* It's good for the economy... She's right... Could we try another design?

GOD: *(He counts on his fingers – two vs. two.)* Oy vey... *(He puts his head in hands.)* This is what happens when you let people decide. *(God thinks, and with authoritative power God takes Truth and throws her to the ground. Smoke, noise of shattering glass. Truth breaks into a thousand jagged pieces. The pieces shine only for a while, for quickly husks grow around each shard, and they are lost from sight.)*
(Hubbub, pandemonium, angels all puzzled and excited)

ANGEL 2: Oh, my God!

GOD: Yes?

ANGEL 3: Look at the pieces.

ANGEL 4: Thousands of them...

ANGEL 3: Jagged.

ANGEL 2: Shining. But wait...

ANGEL 3: Something is growing up around the pieces.

ANGEL 4: Covering them up.

ANGEL 2. Husks. There are husks growing up around the pieces.

ANGEL 3: Oh, almighty, why did you destroy your emblem, Truth?

GOD: "Let Truth spring up from the earth," I once said. *(To a puzzled angel.)* Psalms 85, 11, kid.

The election is over. Finito. It's 2:1. Let there be man and woman! And... let them look for truth.

(Cymbals, drums. Becoming weaker as God speaks, now with feeling, sympathy.)

Don't touch them, angels. Let the shards of our beautiful, shining truth remain hidden. Let them mix with the earth. Men, women, their children...they will find them. In their time. Some will rip off the husks, and be blinded. They will think "I have it now, I understand." Some will touch the shards carefully, and will feel, only feel, that the truth... is not simple. That everyone only has a piece of it. That they need the others, to reassemble my truth. Give them time, my angels.

(After a pause, God looks to the side of the stage, gestures.)

There they go, man and woman, hand in hand, into the garden.

(God sighs, there slowly mounts a drum roll. God turns, and speaks with authority)

Send an e-mail to Satan.

(Stage hands rush into pick up the shards, in view of the audience.)

END OF SCENE

SCENE 2

Pressner house 1992, shifting to 1943 Gribniv attic. Frieda and Emile. In attic there's a 49-year younger Frieda and Emile, Myroslav Olesko's head and body might be seen, but he doesn't speak.

Frieda is lying in bed, but can't seem to find a comfortable spot. She moans from time to time.

EMILE: Are you OK, mammi?

FRIEDA: My bones hurt.

EMILE: Would you like me to get you a Tylenol?

FRIEDA: No, it won't help. *(She is quiet for a moment.)* We didn't have Tylenol then.

EMILE: *(Thinks.)* You mean in the war?

FRIEDA: In forty three. We had nothing. Half a suitcase. You don't remember?

EMILE: I was six.

FRIEDA: You were five when we went in, six when we came out. With a father when you went in. Then they killed him. Oooh *(She moans.)*

EMILE: Rest, mammi.

FRIEDA: Nothing. No meat for you.

EMILE: I'm OK. I remember some cold borscht.

FRIEDA: With a few bones in it.

EMILE: That was the way it had to be. Olesko probably didn't have any for his family. *(Pause.)* It tasted good, mammi. Even if the one you make now is better.

FRIEDA: *(Not listening to him.)* Nothing. No medicine for my brother.

She tosses, eventually settles down. Emile covers her with a blanket, pats her, goes out of room quietly.

The light, dim, switches to the 1943 attic. In the attic a younger Frieda is sleeping, behind her perhaps the dim shape of a man, in front a little boy, the young Emile.

The action that follows is silent. A trap door opens, with strong light from below. A man's head appears. Frieda jumps up. The boy stirs, sits up. Frieda signals to the man to wait, goes over to Emile, pats him, he settles down. The man climbs up a little higher, but never into the attic. He lifts up a pail, Frieda takes it (Light from below is on her.) She hands him another pail, which obviously smells bad. The man goes down, Frieda looks after him. He comes back up with two bottles, maybe filled with water, and then a covered pot. Finally, he brings up a newspaper. He says something, Frieda smiles, talks quietly to him. The child stirs. The hatch closes.

Frieda settles Emile, covers him with a blanket. Pats him. She lies down.

END OF SCENE

SCENE 3

1992 Pressner house. Family after dinner, Frieda, Emile, Tamar, Danny, Heather. Some people are having tea, some water; some are sitting, some standing.

Frieda tries to sip her tea through a sugar cube. It dissolves. She makes a face and takes another sugar cube. She pushes the bowl away, in frustration. The others in the family look at her, smile.

DANNY: Pappa, can I have the Ukrainian stamps on that letter?

EMILE: *(Startled.)* What letter, Danny?

DANNY: The one in your office.

EMILE: How did you see that letter?

TAMAR: What letter?

DANNY: I couldn't find my dictionary, so I went in (*He points to office offstage.*) to borrow yours. It was under it.

HEATHER: Ukrainian?

DANNY: Yeh. I recognized the stamps, a girl in them. It's their first stamps after they became a country again. Maybe they're worth something.

TAMAR: What's the letter about, Emile?

EMILE: *(Uncomfortable, resigned.)* I'll get it.
(He goes off in the direction Danny pointed to earlier.)

HEATHER: The Ukraine is where you came from, grandma, wasn't it?

FRIEDA: Those murderers.

(The others look at her, but not for long. Maybe they've heard her say it before.)

TAMAR: I thought it was Poland.

FRIEDA: First Austria-Hungary, then Poland, when Emile was born. Then the Russians took it. Now it's Ukraine. Let them have it.   *(Emile comes back, holding the letter.)*

EMILE: Here it is. *(He hands it to Tamar.)*

TAMAR: *(Turns it over, sees it has been opened.)* I can't read it.

HEATHER: *(Takes letter.)* I think it's in Russian.

EMILE: No, Ukrainian.

TAMAR: *(Takes letter back.)* The address is in English. It's for Frieda. *(She looks up at Emile, starting to say something [Why didn't you…] then changes her mind.)*   When did that come, Emile?

EMILE: *(Looking guilty.)* Oh, last week, maybe.

TAMAR: So why didn't you give it to your mother?

EMILE: She can't read it.

TAMAR: She reads Ukrainian better than you, I bet.

FRIEDA: *(Who has been following the conversation quietly so far.)* He's right. I can't see.

DANNY: You can see, grandma. You saw me take a popsicle from the refrigerator.

FRIEDA: A little I can see. It's a curse, this macular. I can't read the Inquirer.

TAMAR: You could read the letter for her, Emile.

HEATHER: Can you read Ukrainian, pappa?

EMILE: Yes, I can make it out, most of it at least. I knew Ukrainian once. They were all around us, we lived with them…

FRIEDA: Murderers.

EMILE: But I forgot it. *(He starts to read.)* "*Shanovna Pani* Frieda…" It's the old formal language, "Dear Mrs. Frieda…"

FRIEDA: Who is it from, Emile?

EMILE: Wait a moment. *(He turns letter over to read the signature at the end.)* It says it's from Alla Olesko.

FRIEDA: Olesko. From Gribniv.

DANNY: Do you know them, grandma?

FRIEDA: Do I know them? They're the people who hid us in '43 and '44.

EMILE: They're not alive, it's their daughter writing.

HEATHER: Hid you? Where?

FRIEDA: It doesn't matter. We paid them. They hid us. *(She turns away.)* I'm tired, Emile. Read the letter, tell me what it says later… *(She limps out.)*

EMILE: I will, mammi.

HEATHER: She never wants to talk about it. I have a project at school, about the Holocaust…

EMILE: Who can blame her, Heather? She lost her father, her husband, her young sister. Let her be.

END OF SCENE

SCENE 4

*1992/1943, Emile as child and adult, the child in the attic.
Begins with Emile as adult speaking, shifts to Emile as child,
then again as an adult. In the transition, lines could be
spoken together:*

EMILE as adult: In the attic, I waited for when the
kids burst out of the schoolhouse. Then I'd tiptoe to the
window. I watched the children playing…

EMILE as child: … but they are always running out
of the window frame. The wood… slats… that's what
mammi called them…don't let me see everything. I
heard the children call Pavel's name. He's the boy who
kicked the ball. But I couldn't see where it ended up. I'm
moving, moving one slat to another, trying to make the
world come out *(Acts this out.)*. Yesterday I saw Teacher
Olesko's wife with a basket go to the left, I saw her come
back with eggs. I could smell them, maybe we'd get a
couple. Once I saw a fat goose, escaped from her pen.
Saved from slaughter, I thought. Once I saw Alla, in her
fancy vest. Why was she dressed up?

I can't see the sky; the slats point down, they can't be
moved. I see the field in back of the school, the out-
house, always the same field, only snow turns into mud
into grass into snow.

EMILE as adult: *(Almost wistfully.)* When we moved to
the storage room downstairs, I couldn't see the children
any more.

END OF SCENE

SCENE 5

1992 Pressner house. Next day. Family after dinner, Frieda, Emile, Tamar, Danny, Heather. We come in in the middle of a conversation.

TAMAR: They have their own country now.

FRIEDA: They can have it. They helped the Germans kill us.

EMILE: And they saved us. One did.

DANNY: That's the people who wrote, right? You know them, grandma?

FRIEDA: Of course we know them. We send them packages.

EMILE: Someone with a Ukrainian name walked into Uncle Ernie's office one day. They got to talking, and it turned out he came from near Gribniv, where we were hidden. We sent them packages, that's what grandma is referring to. In the early days you had to choose from an expensive list the Soviets had – coffee, spam, choco-lates…

FRIEDA: And thread.

EMILE: No, that came later. Grandma is thinking about a time when things got more relaxed, we could ask them what they wanted. In time it was calculators, T-shirts…

FRIEDA: And colored thread.

EMILE: For embroidery, that special Ukrainian black and / red and…

FRIEDA: American thread.

EMILE: Because the Russian colors ran.

FRIEDA: Nothing good there.

EMILE: Mammi, don't exaggerate. Where did your *pierogi* come from?

HEATHER, DANNY: We love *pierogi*… when are you going to make them? *(Grandma smiles.)*

EMILE: Anyway, we've been in touch for more than 35 years now. The man who hid us, and his wife died in the '70s and '80s. We lost contact for a while, but now we're in touch again, with their daughter. A letter a year. And we still send packages. Or money.

HEATHER: Because they saved you?

FRIEDA: Because they saved us. But Daniel, Emile's father, died.

EMILE: That wasn't Olesko's fault.

FRIEDA: No, the Nazis killed him. *Nu*, Emile what did the letter say?

EMILE: It's from his daughter, Alla. She says everything is fine in their family. They're worried what will happen to their pensions in the new Ukraine. And – this is the real news, mammi – Alla is on her way here.

TAMAR: Here?

EMILE: Well, to New York. To Brooklyn, to work, taking care of children in a family. She wants to visit us. She has… something that belongs to us, she says.

(Lights out. Spots on Tamar and Emile downstage)

TAMAR: Emile, you didn't get that letter a week ago. When did it come?

EMILE: Well, *(Hesitates.)* Two months ago.

TAMAR: Two months ago. Why didn't you show it to your mother? It was for her.

EMILE: Because… it would have woken up memories in her.

TAMAR: So?

EMILE: Memories that would be painful.

TAMAR: But the woman, Olesko's daughter. She wants to come. She has something of your mother's. Do you know what it is?

EMILE: No.

TAMAR: So you hid the letter. What would you have done if she came, and we didn't know about it? If she just showed up at the door?

EMILE: I don't know, Tamar. Maybe… I'd tell her mammi is too sick, she can't see her. My mother doesn't need to be reminded of the wartime.

TAMAR: No. It's you to whom the memories would be painful.

END OF SCENE

SCENE 6

1943 Schoolhouse attic. Emile and Frieda. Begins with Emile as adult speaking, shifts to Emile as child, then again to adult. In the transition, lines could be spoken together.

EMILE: *(As adult.)* It was time for me to start learning how to read. But there wasn't much light, only near the window, only in the day. So we sat there, and she read quietly to me. *(Emile and Frieda act out as much as possible of the actions described.)*
I drew, with two pencil stubs. I answered her questions. She was good at making up questions.
There were all these geography books in the attic. It was a school, after all. Simple atlases, green and brown land, blue seas. I loved the mountains, the deserts. We played games. Mammi would ask how you get from Gribniv to San Francisco, and I would have to tell her every sea we passed through, every river, every cape. Without looking in the atlas.

EMILE: *(As child.) (Throughout Emile's account, Frieda nods in encouragement, as appropriate.)* This is what you do, mammi; first you walk out to the road that ends near the church, you wait a while for a peasant to give you a ride, for a few *groshy*, to the main road, the one where you said father built the bridges. There you wait for the bus. In Strody you catch a train — maybe we could visit Grandma Fanny, when the Nazis go. The train goes to Lemberg, we wait a few hours, take another train to Warszawa. Still by train to Gdansk. Then you get on a boat, go out into the Bay of Danzig, the Baltic, through Öresund, Kattegat, and...I forgot the third one.

16

FRIEDA: Let's look it up, son. *(She opens the school atlas.)* What does it say in the atlas?

EMILE: But maybe you can cut across by the Kiel Canal. Am I allowed to do that?

FRIEDA: *(Shakes her head, gently.)* Not this time, Emile.

EMILE: *(Reads.)* Skage…rrak *(May be mispronounced.)*. What funny names around Denmark. Out to the North Sea, through the English Channel, out to the Atlantic. Then, because we have time, like here in the attic, we can sail the longer way — do you want me to tell you all the names of the islands we pass, mammi? *(She nods.)*

Past South America, I wish we could stop in Montevideo, through the straits of Magellan, near — how does one say it? —Tierra del Fuego, up the long coast of Chile and this island of Robinson Crusoe — please, I want you to read that story again — up further, past Panama, where there's a canal that could have saved us time, up this long chicken leg that sticks out of Mexico, to California. Here's a bay, here's San Francisco.

EMILE: *(as adult)* How did I do, mammi, did I get it right, mammi?

END OF SCENE

17

SCENE 7

1992, a week later, Pressner house. Heather and her grand-mother, Frieda.

FRIEDA: Oh, dear Heather. It was a horrible time, OK? That's all one can say. Why do you want to go back to it?

HEATHER: But I have this history course at Germantown Friends, grandma. And I need to write a paper based on the personal experience of someone who's lived through... an important time.

FRIEDA: Feh, important! It wasn't important. For who? No one cared about us.

HEATHER: Please tell me, grandma.

FRIEDA: You wouldn't understand, how can you understand? You've lived here, you're American. These things don't happen here.

HEATHER: Try me, grandma. Let me ask some questions.

FRIEDA: *(Softening.)* So ask already.

HEATHER: I know you grew up in *(She looks at her notes.)* this little town in the Ukraine, Strody.

FRIEDA: They call it Ukraine, those murderers. It was Poland.

HEATHER: I saw it on the map, grandma. Strody is now in the Ukraine. Was it a *shtetl*?

FRIEDA: *(Maybe a little insulted.)* A *shtetl*? Is Philadelphia a *shtetl*? It was a town, 12,000 people – Ukrainians, Jews, Poles. It was a good Polish town. *(She is quiet for a moment.)* The Poles didn't like us much either. When Daniel… your grandfather… went to school at the Polytechnic, the Polish students beat him with razor blades on sticks.

HEATHER: Why?

FRIEDA: Because he was Jewish; they made the Jewish boys sit in ghetto benches.

HEATHER: I don't understand.

FRIEDA: Like blacks in the back of the bus? You've heard about that?

HEATHER: Yes, a long time ago, in the South.

FRIEDA: At the same time, in Poland. The Jewish students had to sit on special benches. *(Bitterly.)* It was the nice Polish students who made them do it. They made a law.

HEATHER: *(Impatient to go on.)* So what happened in the War?

FRIEDA: We had the Russians 1939-41. They and the Nazis divided up Poland. It wasn't a bad time for the Jews. I worked in the office of a Soviet "*nachalnik.*" A boss. Bah – I did all the work, he sat around, spit the *(She hesitates, to find the word.)*…hulls of the sunflower seeds into a drawer. Which a Ukrainian had to clean up.

19

HEATHER: *(Eager to push her grandmother on.)* Then the Germans came.

FRIEDA: You know when?

HEATHER: *(Looks at her notes.)* June 22, 1941.

FRIEDA: *(Smiles.)* Good girl. *(Pause.)* The Nazis came into Strody, and the Ukrainians organized a pogrom. They ran through town, rounding up Jews. I was at work, waited till dark to run home.

HEATHER: Were you OK?

FRIEDA: *(Nods.)* Emile was with my mother. Passing Krakowska I saw some Ukrainians, my classmates, dragging a man, yelling *"Parkhatyi zhid!"*

HEATHER: Par…*(Tries to pronounce it, so she can write it down. She can't. Frieda notices.)*

FRIEDA: "Lousy Jew." It was my cousin Duvid, they beat him with a stick… And I couldn't help him, I had a child. I ran home, but my father was caught, and my brother Motek too.

HEATHER: Uncle Motek?

FRIEDA: They took them to the castle. And shot them. *Einsatzgruppe C.* Your greatgrandfather Berl, and your granduncle Motek. And 3000 others. The Ukrainians brought them there, and the SS killed them.

HEATHER: But uncle Motek is alive!

FRIEDA: He crawled out from under the dead. With a dum-dum bullet in his wrist. To this day he carries it. *(Pause.)* My father… *(She shakes her head.)*

HEATHER: *(Softly.)* So what happened next?

FRIEDA: I can't go on, Heather *(Crying.)* My father… *(Heather and her grandmother hug each other.)*

END OF SCENE

SCENE 8

1992, a day later, Pressner house. Heather, Emile. Frieda walks in during scene.

HEATHER: Pappa, I finally got grandma to talk. About the war. Or part of it.

EMILE: What did she tell you?

HEATHER: More than you ever did. About Strody. How the Soviets came in '39. That it wasn't so bad then.

EMILE: Did she tell you about her sunflower-spitting boss?

HEATHER: She did. *(Beat.)* I've seen you eat those seeds.

EMILE: At least I don't spit them in the drawer.

HEATHER: Then she stopped talking, right at the 1941 pogrom. She couldn't go on.

EMILE: It's hard for her.

HEATHER: Maybe you can tell me.

EMILE: I was 4 years old in 1941, Heather. I was not quite 7 when the war ended for us in 1944.

HEATHER: But you have to remember something!

EMILE: A little. My memory is bad. *(Pause.)* But I know what she told me.

HEATHER: Which you never tell us. Danny and I ask you all the time.

EMILE: Danny is a child. And so were you.

HEATHER: I'm ten years older than you were at the end of the war!

EMILE: It was a terrible time.

HEATHER: That's exactly what grandma said. But you both lived through it. If you don't remember, what did grandma tell you? What did Uncle Ernie tell you? *(At this point, Frieda walks in slowly, limping, sits down at the table.)*

EMILE: *(Slowly.)* We stayed in the house in town for a while. And then went into the labor camp, It was a way to stay out of the ghetto.

HEATHER: Why did you want to do that? Wasn't the labor camp worse?

EMILE: No. Because in '42 they began shipping people off from the ghetto, to work they said. To kill them.

FRIEDA: One came back, he jumped off a train. He told us they gassed them in Sobibor.

EMILE: You told me it was Belzec, mammi. And no one came back from there.

FRIEDA: It was Sobibor.

EMILE: *(Wants to object, then stops.)*

FRIEDA: No one wanted to believe him, but your father did. In the camp things were better. That's why we went there. Only one German beast, Warzok. He beat me *(She points to her shoulder.)* The others – Romanians, Slovaks, Lithuanians – we could pay. Emile was in the camp. No children were supposed to be there, but the guards looked the other way. My Daniel – he could go in and out.

EMILE: My father could do this because he was an engineer. He built the bridges that the Russians bombed and the camp was rebuilding. The Germans needed him.

FRIEDA: We bought our way out of that camp. Paid the guards. One night we walked out, to Olesko's school in Gribniv. He was the teacher in the village; he lived in the school.

EMILE: Mammi, I always wondered how you and my father got to these people.

FRIEDA. We knew someone in their family. When the camp was working nearby, your father talked to Olesko. Everyone was looking for a place to hide. So we came to the house, and went into the attic. And stayed there. Emile was 5 when we went in.

HEATHER: How long were you in there?

FRIEDA: Fifteen months. Every day we looked death in the eye.

END OF SCENE

SCENE 9

1992, attic, Frieda. Emile, possibly, in a silent role.

FRIEDA: They ask me if I have nightmares. *(Pause.)*

Who needs nightmares? I lie there at night. I think of something good, Danny up to some prank, sticking matches into his mother's *shabbes* candles. As if I didn't see him. Heather, what a beauty. American kids.

And then I think of Emile in the attic. It was good he was a quiet child.

(In what follows there could be a prop serving as the dog house, and Emile could climb up on it. If he is there, he can say "bang, bang" after "they started shooting.")

One day, in the camp, before we went into the attic, two SS men came in late, as it was getting dark. A little drunk. They said they needed a little shooting practice. To scare us, I think... They put Emile, who was 4, on top of a dog house, and told him to keep quiet. Then they walked back a few meters, pulled out their guns. "Don't worry, miss, we just want him to have a good view when we shoot the dog," one said. The other one broke up in laughter. "So what if Klaus misses!" More laughter. They made me watch. They started shooting – the dog barked, ran out. They shot him, a few centimeters from Emile. *(Through her teeth.) "Das war ein grosser Spass."* Great fun.

Emile just looked at me. Thank God he was a quiet child.

END OF SCENE

SCENE 10

1992, two days later. Grandma's room in Pressner house. Frieda is lying down, Emile pacing around.

EMILE: Mammi, why didn't you ever nominate Olesko to be one of the Righteous Among the Nations? [1]

FRIEDA: Why should I?

EMILE: Because he saved us. And Uncle Ernie.

FRIEDA: We paid them.

EMILE: How did you pay them?

FRIEDA: What do you think? In gold. The only thing that was worth something. First with coins, we had some Swiss ones. Then, when the coins ran out, with jewelry. *(She looks at her fingers, bare of rings.)* Do you have some gold?

EMILE: *(Startled.)* Gold. Why? No.

FRIEDA: You should have some. You should always have some gold around the house.

EMILE: Mammi, this is America.

FRIEDA: You never know.

EMILE: *(Shaking his head.)* It doesn't matter that you paid him. It was a great risk – he and his family, his small children…

FRIEDA: They would have killed them. We looked at death every day. One night, Warzok, the beast, rode into the village. The one who beat me *(She touches her back, shudders.)*. I felt it.

EMILE: So why not have this good man recognized? *Yad vaShem* / wants to honor…

FRIEDA: *(Interrupts.)* Because they would kill him.

EMILE: Who? Who now? After the war!

FRIEDA: Emile, you don't understand. In that village, Gribniv, after the war, they somehow found out Olesko hid some Jews. They beat him up. They shot him in the leg.

EMILE: How do you know that?

FRIEDA: He told us later, in a letter taken out by someone, not through the mail.

EMILE: Because he hid Jews?

FRIEDA: *(Shakes her head no.)* You don't know what kind of people they are.

EMILE: So why?

FRIEDA: *(Angry.)* Because they thought he had money. That's all, money. Because he hid Jews.

EMILE: I think you're crazy, mammi. Maybe right after the war. *(Pause.)* But then the Russians stopped all that. That at least they did well.

FRIEDA: It's not good to be a good *goy* among murderers.

EMILE: You said it. He was a good man. He saved us. He's not alive; no one can shoot him now.

FRIEDA: They'll shoot his children. Ask your uncle.

EMILE: I asked him. He thought for a while, said "Leave things alone." I don't know what he meant. He said, "You don't know these people." I think he meant the people in the village, just like you.

FRIEDA: They'll never change.

END OF SCENE

SCENE 11

1992, Frieda, in her room. Or in attic.

FRIEDA: I had a dream. There's a woman trapped under a grate. She spoke to me, quietly, asking for help. We must save her. But move slowly, for she's grown in there, grown to the shape of the sewer. Her bones must be bent, we can't just take her out. Her muscles have to be massaged. Before we walked out, in June forty four, walked from Olesko's house to the Russian lines, didn't I massage Ernie's legs? Women are stronger. They were swollen, his legs, there was no place to walk in the storeroom where we hid, the bunker we dug under it. *(Pause.)*
We have to lift her out gently, with oil poured round her, with a winch, there's time. Please talk to her, ask her how she came in the sewer, why her children left her, was there a time she could lift the grate. Ask her what food people threw her way; where her patience came from. And who else lived in the sewers, and did she learn rat language. Meanwhile, I'll get help.

END OF SCENE

SCENE 12

1992, night of same day as preceding 1992 scene between Emile and Frieda. Place anywhere in Pressner house. Emile and Tamar.

EMILE: I ask her why she didn't nominate him for one of the Righteous Among the Nations, and she says: "They would have shot him!"

TAMAR: Who would have shot him?

EMILE: That's what I asked. The other people in the village, she says. Because they think he got money from the Jews he hid.

TAMAR: Well, you paid him.

EMILE: It wasn't much.

TAMAR: Enough, in that simple village. And what does Uncle Ernie say?

EMILE: He said something a little different. "Leave things alone."

TAMAR: Hmm. *(Thinks.)* So they both don't want to put in that nomination.

EMILE: I think they are stuck in some wild ideas about the past. And I think they are going to regret it one day.

TAMAR: Why?

EMILE: Because we didn't thank them. You put it off, you put it off, and it begins to eat at you. Because the people who saved us deserve thanks.

TAMAR: Maybe there's something else behind this.

EMILE: Like what?

TAMAR: A reason they can't bring themselves to say.

EMILE: Like what?

TAMAR: Oh, Emile, you are so naïve. Haven't you read about what happened in those days?

EMILE: I don't have any idea what you are talking about.

TAMAR: Maybe Olesko wasn't as good as you, the little boy you were, thought he was. Your mother was 32, an attractive woman…

EMILE: *(Long pause.)* No, I don't think it's possible.

TAMAR: Why not ask her one day?

EMILE: You want me, her son, to ask her if… if he… if she…

TAMAR: No, I take it back. You can't ask her. And maybe no one can, *(Beat.)* or should. I don't know what took place — people did… things to save their lives. *(Pause.)* That's the German's worst crime, what they made people do. *(Silence.)* I'm just thinking of reasons for her and Ernie's hesitation.

EMILE: It's not fair he's not recognized.

TAMAR: I think it's <u>you</u> who need the peace of thanks, Emile. *(Pause.)* One day, when she dies, you'll nominate him.

END OF SCENE

31

SCENE 13

1943 attic. Emile as a child, the younger Frieda. Both are sitting on the floor, in the dim light of the window.

FRIEDA: I've thought up a new game.

EMILE: An entirely new game?

FRIEDA: Yes, I read about it in a book. First we draw these circles on the floor. Six in front of you, six in front of me. Got it, Emile? *(Emile draws the circles, laboriously, on a piece of cardboard, with a pencil stub his mother hands him. He holds it up, looks at her for approval. Which she gives, drawing her own circles next.)* Great! Now a bigger one on each side of the six. *(They both draw.)* That's called a *(Slowly.)* man-ca-la.

EMILE: That doesn't sound Polish, mammi.

FRIEDA: It's not, it's African.

EMILE: *(Makes a connection.)* Mammi, can you read me *In Desert and Wilderness* again? About Staś and Nell.[2] *(Excited.)* That's in Africa too.

FRIEDA: Shhh. Yes, of course, I'll read it for you. From the beginning. But now we need some things to play with, little pebbles, buttons.

EMILE: Where are we going to get those?

FRIEDA: *(Thinks.)* Go get your pillow. Quietly. *(Emile goes to get it, on tiptoes, avoiding a piece of the floor that creaks.)* Bring it here. *(He does.)* I am going to take out some peas. *(She begins to untie a knot in the simple pillow.)*

EMILE: *(Worried.)* No, mammi, I won't be able to sleep.

FRIEDA: You'll sleep just fine, Emile, you won't miss the ones we need. *(She thinks.)* Yes, we can also try to count how many there are left.
(Pause, as she unties the knots in the pillow full of peas.)
Pappa is coming Sunday.
(Frieda unties the bag and takes about 40 peas out. Emile looks suspicious)

EMILE: It's going to feel flat.

FRIEDA: You silly. *(She gives him a hug.)* Put 4 peas in each circle. But not in the mancalas. That's where we are going to store our winnings.

EMILE: *(With a big smile.)* But am I allowed to eat the ones I win?

FRIEDA: *(Smiles back.)* Of course you can. Hard dried peas. I bet they taste wonderful.

EMILE: And pappa is coming soon.

END OF SCENE

SCENE 14

1992, a few days later. Pressner house. Heather and her grandmother, Frieda.

HEATHER: Pappa said I should ask you about when you were a child, before the War.

FRIEDA: Another war.

HEATHER: What do you mean?

FRIEDA: You know there was World War II. This was World War I. I was born in 1911, before that war. Lucky me, two wars.

HEATHER: What happened in that war?

FRIEDA: We were first run over by the Russians. My father, Berl, may he rest in peace, got taken prisoner. Off to Siberia. This was 1915. My mother was taking my two older brothers and me with Lidia, our Ukrainian nanny, somewhere, God knows where. On a train. We were stopped in Lemberg by some fighting. My mother went down to find some food in town. Just then the Austrians attacked. We got separated by the front lines.

HEATHER: You were four, grandma.

FRIEDA: A little girl, a *sheine meydele*; my brothers were 6 and 9. Lidia, the nanny, took us slowly to Vienna. She loved us, she didn't let anyone touch us a hair on our head. She slept with the soldiers for bread and milk for us, she begged for sausage and a piece of fruit. We didn't go hungry. *(Pause.)* I loved her, I can see her before my eyes. *(Pause.)* In Vienna, the Red Cross put us in a convent.

HEATHER: Didn't you mother come and get you?

FRIEDA: She was on the other side of the front line. She didn't know we were alive, we didn't know how to reach her. The Red Cross found her. But by then the war was over.

HEATHER: You didn't see your mother for three years?

FRIEDA: *(Shakes her head yes.)* It was the war. The nuns were good to us. *(Pause.)* I loved one especially. *(She feels her breast.)* I have a scar here. Maybe you saw it. *(Heather shakes her head no.)* One day this nun came in carrying a big kettle of hot chicken soup. I ran to her, I wanted to hug her. The kettle spilled over me, I had terrible burns. *(She cringes.)*

HEATHER: And your Ukrainian nanny, what happened to her?

FRIEDA: I don't know. It was the war.

END OF SCENE

SCENE 15

1943, Frieda alone, attic. A kerosene lamp.

FRIEDA: He didn't come that Sunday. I knew something was wrong. I begged Olesko to find out. He asked around, the camp was very quiet, he said. Too quiet. The guards said they took some people to town.

A week later a letter came, Olesko said it was slipped under the door at night. From an engineer friend of Daniel's. It told the story, how they tortured Daniel, killed him, against a wall.

I should have kept him from going back, I should have tried harder. *(She cries.)*

I tried not to cry, only when Emile slept, only when he cried.

What risks people took to bring those letters to us! And Olesko is scared, too many people know we are here.

I will write to Daniel, *(Pause.)* in his notebook, the one he wrote in. *(She leafs through it. Reads.)* "We may compare the earth with such a moving vehicle, in the course around… the sun… *(She begins to break down)* which in the course around the sun has a remarkable speed…" *(Pause, as she collects herself.)* He's taking notes, writing down what he reads on relativity theory. He's doing this in the camp. In German.

I should have kept him from going back.

END OF SCENE

SCENE 16

1992, two days later. Pressner house. Danny, Emile, Frieda, perhaps in kitchen.

DANNY: Pappa, there's something I don't understand. Grandma keeps saying that the Ukrainians helped the Nazis, that they were worse than the Nazis. But why? Why would the Ukrainians have it in for the Jews?

EMILE: The Ukrainians were antisemitic.

TAMAR: Antisemitic is not enough, Emile. Many Poles didn't like the Jews either. Your mother has some good stories on this, like the students that tortured her husband.

FRIEDA: There was no reason. They hated us. For centuries – remember Chmelnitsky's pogroms.

EMILE: Maybe there was… a piece of a reason. In their minds. In 1941. Only in their minds.

TAMAR: What?

EMILE: If I tell it to you, it will sound like I'm excusing the Ukrainians. And there is no excuse for what they did.

FRIEDA: The murderers.

DANNY: Tell us anyway, pappa. *(Silence.)*

EMILE: The Soviets shot all the Ukrainians in the castle the week before.

DANNY: I don't get it, pappa. Why were the Russians

killing Ukrainians?

TAMAR: And what does that have to do with the Ukrainians hating the Jews? Before, before when?

EMILE: *(Sighing.)* I know it's complicated. OK, a little time line: In 1939, the Germans and Russians, buddies for a while, carve up Poland. Strody falls into the Soviet zone. Got it, Danny?

DANNY: Sort of…

EMILE: The Ukrainians in the region don't like the Soviets at all. They want an independent Ukraine. The NKVD, the Soviet secret police, had it in for the Ukrainian nationalists. Or Ukrainians they thought were nationalists.

FRIEDA: They all were.

EMILE: So the NKVD puts hundreds of Ukrainians into a prison at the castle above Strody. All the Ukrainian doctors, teachers, the leaders of their community. It's June 1941. Just then the Germans attack. It will take them a week to reach Strody. In that week, the Soviet secret police in the castle, instead of fighting, shoots the Ukrainian prisoners,

DANNY: Oof.

EMILE: Every one of them, buries them in a mass grave in the castle courtyard.

FRIEDA: Just a few. It was the war.

EMILE: No not a few. Six hundred and fifty. Probably

some of your classmates, mammi, people you knew.

TAMAR: But again, what does that have to do with the Jews?

EMILE: This is where the story gets crazy. Many of the Soviet NKVD – the secret police that killed the Ukrainians — were Jewish. That's what the Ukrainians said. They say it still. Today.

DANNY: Were they? Were they Jewish?

EMILE: There were Jews in the NKVD, sure. There were Ukrainians in the NKVD too. But that most of the NKVD were Jews — that was a lie.

FRIEDA: A lie, like everything they say.

EMILE: That lie got mixed up with Ukrainian anti-semitism, deep and old. And with images of some Jews welcoming the Soviets, when they marched in two years before.

DANNY: Did they welcome them? The Jews, I mean.

FRIEDA: I didn't.

EMILE: Some did. But most Jews were as far from Communists as you can imagine. There were right wing types, religious, merchants. Loyal Poles. None of them liked the Soviets.

FRIEDA: Don't forget. 3000 they killed that first week. With Ukrainian help.

EMILE: She's talking about the Nazis.

DANNY: Pappa says the Ukrainians had a reason to help.

FRIEDA: Danny!

EMILE: You see why I didn't want to tell you this story. There is no excuse for what the Ukrainians did.

TAMAR: It was the SS that did the killing. And if it were not for the war…

FRIEDA: The Ukrainians helped them.

TAMAR: Not all Ukrainians, Frieda. *(She stops.)* If the Nazis hadn't been there / it wouldn't have happened…

FRIEDA: They would have found another excuse for a pogrom.

EMILE: *(Pause.)* The Ukrainians were drunk, on a poisonous brew. Drunk on hate.

TAMAR: The war…*(She can't go on. A silence envelops them all).*

Lights out.
Spot on Emile and Frieda downstage.

EMILE: Mammi, Alla called. Olesko's daughter. She's coming next week.

FRIEDA: What does she want, Emile? She wrote she had something of ours.

EMILE: You remembered.

FRIEDA: What could she have? *(She shakes her head.)* We came there with a small suitcase, we left with nothing.

END OF SCENE

SCENE 17

1943 Attic, Begins with Emile as adult speaking, shifts to Emile as child, then again toward adult. In the transitions lines could be spoken together.

(There is the possibility of acting out the cupping, with Frieda and a silent actor as Ernie. Or Frieda alone.)

EMILE AS ADULT: At night Olesko let him into the attic; and the strong uncle from the forest, who gave the guns to my father, who has a gun, my uncle Ernie, climbs into the attic with his last strength. He lies senseless with a fever; two days pass, there is no medicine, just herbs, no doctor to be trusted. The fever didn't break. They put me to bed. My mother asks Olesko for some glasses, some jam jars, a spirit lamp.

EMILE AS CHILD: But I pretend to sleep, watch. Something different is going to happen tonight. They cover the window with two cloths. They light a lamp, one kerosene, one a small spirit lamp. *(He pauses.)* We never had two lamps before. She bares his back, heats the glasses one after the other over the small lamp — jam jars, big glasses. And with a face I don't recognize, she puts them on his back, He squirms – they burn. Mammi puts a gag in his mouth. One by one, mammi puts the glasses on him. She tries to hold them with a rag, but they slip out, so she uses her hands. Two shatter, they burn her hand. I watch in the lamp light, they forget about me. I watch his flesh and blood rise inside the glasses; red, red welts bright on his back, as the glasses fall off. And Uncle Ernie falls, sweating, asleep.

My mother cries – holds me.

EMILE AS ADULT: It was the only thing she knew she could do, and she hurt him.

END OF SCENE

SCENE 18

1992, two days later, Pressner house. Emile and Tamar, setting unimportant.

EMILE: She just can't stop talking about the murderers.

TAMAR: And weren't they?

EMILE: Yes, some were. But look who she is talking about. Not the Nazis, but the Ukrainians.

TAMAR: They too.

EMILE: But it was a Ukrainian who saved us.

TAMAR: Oh, Emile. I don't want to take her side, I don't want to be there with all that hate…*(Pause.)* Coming out of all that pain. But I listen; I can understand why she hates the Ukrainians more than the Germans.

EMILE: Why?

TAMAR: You told me yourself. The SS didn't know who was Jewish. The Jews spoke Polish, they spoke Ukrainian. Some didn't look like Jews at all. They looked like Danny and Heather, our blond kids. The Ukrainians gave them away.

EMILE: But look at the risk Olesko took. His schoolhouse was right in the middle of the village, the only brick house...

TAMAR: There weren't many who did what he did.

EMILE: Enough of them. Thousands survived, just as we did.

TAMAR: *(Exasperated.)* Oh Emile. Sometimes I don't know what the attic did to you. *(Quiets down as she begins. But then her exasperation mounts.)*

"Thousands survived." And so many more didn't. *(Beat.)* Each of you, those who are here today, has a story to tell. The stories are uplifting, good for Holocaust Remembrance Day. Each story has a… saviour. A rescuer. Honest men and women, good Christians, maybe even lovers of Jews. But have you ever thought how many stories are missing? How many were turned away from a place to hide? How many were hidden, and then given out? How many did not live to tell their story, a story of betrayal? Who will speak for the dead, Emile? Who will tell their stories?

END OF SCENE

SCENE 19

1992, Emile, Frieda, perhaps in kitchen.

EMILE: Why don't I remember more about my father, Mammi?

FRIEDA: You were five when he was killed. How can you remember? And in the last year, you didn't see much of him. He came to us at night, once a month, maybe. He left before it was light.

EMILE: Once he brought me some candy. I remember that.

FRIEDA: How much money that cost him! You don't know. *(Pause. Then with intensity.)* I will never forgive him.

EMILE: *(Shocked.)* He's dead, mammi. What won't you forgive him for? The candy?

FRIEDA: I begged him to stay with us in the attic. I begged.

EMILE: But he had to go back. He was the only person who could smuggle weapons into the camp. You told me so.

FRIEDA: I told you so…

EMILE: The people were counting on him./ He was…

FRIEDA: The people, sure. The people. They meant more to him than I did, than you did.

EMILE: But they needed him.

FRIEDA: We needed him.

EMILE: Pappa was a hero.

FRIEDA: Now you're back to five years old. Grow up. *(Sarcastic.)* A hero.

EMILE: Yes, you told me many times he was one.

FRIEDA: What about me, Emile?

EMILE: What about you?

FRIEDA: I was left alone. Left alone in the war. Left to take care of you, to nurse Ernie, to pay Olesko. That's what he left me with. And he… he became a hero, for you, for those who survived. For the Israelis. For he fought, when others walked quietly into the cattle cars. They could be proud of their Daniel. After the war. But in '43 I didn't need a hero. I needed my husband.

END OF SCENE

SCENE 20

1992, next day. Kitchen in Pressner house. Emile, Alla and Frieda sit around the table. Alla has Russian clothes on, maybe a poor quality print fabric.

EMILE: It's so good you could come, Alla. It's not easy to take the train from New York…

FRIEDA: Ask her if she wants another piece of cake.

EMILE: *(Quietly.)* Mammi, you can ask her yourself. She understands Polish – she's my age, they kept speaking it in Strody.

ALLA: The hard part was going from the train station here. Philadelphia is not Brooklyn.

FRIEDA: A piece of *mohn strudel,*³ Pani Alla?

ALLA: Oh, thank you. You know your cake is as good as the one my mother made.

FRIEDA: But this one is American.

EMILE: Mammi…

FRIEDA: The dough's better.

ALLA: Pani Frieda / I brought…

FRIEDA: Some more tea?

ALLA: *(Nods. Emile pours her some tea.)* Thank you.

FRIEDA: In Strody, do you still have the *Konditorei* run by the Makowka family?

ALLA: No, the Poles left after the war. Someone else tried to run it. But there was no white flour for a while, no sugar.

FRIEDA: No sugar beets?

ALLA: The Russians took them, and the peasants just grew enough for themselves.

FRIEDA: I remember raspberries rolled in sugar and left to dry. I remember… mother asking me to break off a piece of sugar from the cone, with hammer and chisel.

ALLA: So she could sip her tea through the sugar.

FRIEDA: How did you know that?

ALLA: *(Smiles.)* An old Ukrainian custom.

FRIEDA: I thought it was a Jewish one…

ALLA: *(Stands up.)* Pani Frieda. We think we have something that belongs to you.

FRIEDA: *(Determined.)* No, you don't.

ALLA: Looking through my mother Maria's things – she died after my father, only five years ago – we found in a box some jewelry… *(Alla rummages in her pocketbook. While she does that, the next lines are dialogue spoken aside, between Frieda and Emile.)*

FRIEDA: Her mother didn't want us to stay.

EMILE: Shh, mammi. You don't know that.

FRIEDA: I know it. She gave him trouble.

EMILE: She had 3 little kids; maybe she was worried about people finding out that Jews were hidden in her house.

FRIEDA: She was worried… What about us?

ALLA: *(She takes out a small box, and out of it some tissue paper. She opens the paper, and takes out a gold ring, hands it to Frieda, who stands up to get it.)* It's not my mother's size, she was a big woman. We think it is yours.

(The next actions need to be played slowly. Frieda takes the ring, rolls it once around, and gives the ring to Emile, who now is also standing.)

EMILE: A gold ring. *(Emile turns the ring round, sees something engraved on the inside of the band.)* It has initials in it, F, I think, and *(Pause.)* D. And a date between them Did you use… to pay… Mammi… (His voice trails off; but he is not going to get any help from his mother.) Could that be? *(Pause.)* Is it? *(He swallows.)* Was it… your wedding ring? *(After a moment, Frieda reaches out slowly for the ring. Emile hands it back to Frieda. Who in one motion gives it to Alla.)*

FRIEDA: It's yours.
(Emile reaches out his hand to touch his mother. He understands, all of a sudden. Frieda continues to look into Alla's eyes. Alla hesitates, slowly puts the ring away.)

Lights Out

END OF SCENE

END OF ACT 1

ACT 2

SCENE 21

Same setting as Scene 1, somewhere, in heaven. No Attributes now, just angels. Only five actors are needed in this scene. God (Groucho Marx or Mae West) is sitting at a baroque desk, while angels are scurrying in and out bringing to him/her small vials or flasks with a tiny amount of a shimmering liquid inside. God looks at each flask in turn, says something, an angel records his/her judgment. From time to time God takes a sip from a big bottle of Gatorade. Each of the angels is wearing a T-shirt. One says "Zeek Power". Another says "Made in Heaven: 5770 Tour," a third one, "Brooklyn Dodgers," a fourth one, "Ex-Pre-Med."

GOD: Strong, brunette, pretty smart.

ANGEL 1: *(Repeats)* Strong, brunette, pretty smart.

GOD: Next, please.

ANGEL 2: *(Places next flask in front of God.)* This looks like a good one.

GOD: *(Looks at flask, shakes it.)* Will disappoint his mother by not becoming a doctor. Bad temper, too. But good in bed.

ANGEL 3: God, don't you get tired of this?

GOD: I do, my child. But it's in the job description. Like the President – he has to sign all the officer's commissions. You should see what Queen Elizabeth has to do. *(He takes a swig of Gatorade.)* But I'm worried about you, my children. All this flying back and forth, to get a drop here, a drop there.

ANGEL 1: Thanks for your concern, God. *(Pause.)* It's a pain.

ANGEL 2: You see, there was a time we just had to look at the semen.

ANGEL 3: But then those damned scientists told us it ain't just the male gism.

ANGEL 4: So we have to bring you both the sperm and the egg. You know, after they get together. *(He acts it out in gestures.)*

ANGEL 1: There isn't much time, because it starts dividing…

ANGEL 2: So you can decide what will come of the kid.

ANGEL 4: And while there's a whole division of us…

ANGEL 1: *(Proudly.)* The Zygoteseekers.

ANGEL 2: Zeeks for short.

ANGEL 3: *(Flexes his muscles; shows off Zeek Power T-shirt.)*

ANGEL 4: Frankly, God, it's not ideal working conditions. First we're not wanted in there. Not just then. *(He makes lewd gestures.)*

ANGEL 1: And it's closed in, wet. Lots of noise.

GOD: Where angels fear to tread.

ANGELS: Cheap shot… Alexander Pope… Boo…He's been reading E.M. Forster

GOD: OK, enough griping. It's in a day's, sorry, night's work.

ANGEL 2: I do want to ask a question.

GOD: *(Huffs up.)* It's not your place to ask the master of the universe.

ANGELS: *(Not all together.)* But we're in this together… You want us to help you?…Have you seen what Satan is paying?

GOD: *(Resigned to benevolent.)* OK, *bubbi*. Go ahead, ask.

ANGEL 1: So, God, you decide if a person will be a wise man or a fool.

GOD: Indeed.

ANGEL 2: A soldier or a rabbi.

GOD: Yep.

ANGEL 3: If she will die at 30, or at 80.

GOD: You bet.

ANGEL 4: Will get to Tierra del Fuego or not.

GOD: I do, I do. So get to the point, kids.

ANGEL 1: But you don't say if the man…

ANGEL 2: ..or woman…

ANGEL 3: will be righteous…

ANGEL 4: or evil.

GOD: *(Determined.)* You bet.

ANGELS: So why?

GOD: Because.

ANGELS: *(Not all at once, but interrupting hubbub.)* There he goes again… Next, he'll claim it's not ours to know his ways… *(Singing.)* Because, oh because… Not a good teacher…

GOD: I'll let you figure it out. Why? Why would I, omnithis, omnithat *(A few notes from Handel's Messiah.)* not decide if this mortal should be good, that one evil? And that's the only thing I don't decide? *(Angels are perplexed.)*

GOD: *Nu? Talk to me, (Through the answers, God nods, with the feeling of "How stupid can these angels be?")*

ANGEL1: I hate these questions. They make me feel stupid.

ANGEL 2: I'll have a go. *(Pause.)* Because it's no fun to decide everything ahead of time?

ANGEL 3: Because you messed up programming that?

ANGEL 4: There wouldn't be college courses on free will and determinism?

GOD: *(To audience.)* You see what help they give me? *(More seriously, slowly.)* Because I keep hoping something came from that seed I put in the rice paddy, the seed that in God's time became them. Something more than molecules. Because I like risk. Because I love them.

END OF SCENE

SCENE 22

In attic, 1943. No one speaks in this scene. Emile, Frieda

Emile is standing by the window, looking out, shifting to see the children playing. Frieda is worried that he might jar the slats, tries to get him away from the window. Emile does not want to go. She shows him an atlas, and motions to him to come to her. He trips, his mother catches him. But there was a bang, his knee hit the floor, and they all freeze, waiting to hear if anyone heard them. Emile wants to go back to the window, but his mother holds him to her.

Frieda takes out a deck of cards, and encourages Emile in gestures to build a house of the cards. He tries, a few times, but the cards fall down. Frieda tries to help him, but he still can't get it. He gets frustrated. Frieda draws him into a hug, to quiet him down. She points to a page in the atlas, tells him to draw it on a piece of paper. Begins to draw a continent, some rivers. There is a knock on the trapdoor to the attic.

END OF SCENE

SCENE 23

1992, downstage, right after last scene of Act1. Spot on Emile and Alla.

EMILE: Alla, there's something I wanted to ask you. Let me walk with you to the train.

ALLA: Please don't trouble yourself, *Pan* Emile.

EMILE: Please call me Emile. We're the same age. And actually that is related to what I wanted to talk to you about.

ALLA: Yes?

EMILE: You see I have this memory. *(Pause.)* My memory is not too good… of those times.

ALLA: They were not good times.

EMILE: I remember… that you and I played together, for a day or two. In clear sunlight. Except… it doesn't make sense, Alla. We came into your house at night, so that no one would see us. And we didn't come out till the Russians came back. Not for one day, one night in those 15 months. *(Pause.)*
I asked my mother about it, and she said, that's right, we didn't come out.

ALLA: But we did play, *Pan* Emile.

EMILE: How could we?

ALLA: We did. Except it wasn't while you were hidden. *(Pause.)* I didn't know you were in the attic.

EMILE: You never heard us?

ALLA: Not that I remember. Children don't pay much attention to noises.

EMILE: *(Smiling.)* Not even ghosts? Ghosts in the attic?

ALLA: You must have been very quiet. *(Pause.)* But we did play, after.

EMILE: How could we?

ALLA: You came back, after the Nazis left and the Russians came, after you went back to Strody. To take some things you left in the attic, I guess.

EMILE: *(Amazed.)* I don't remember that.

ALLA: But you remember playing?

EMILE: I do.

ALLA: You stayed a day or two. It was a beautiful fall day, I remember it.

EMILE: It was in the forest, up the hillside behind the school.

ALLA: We built a… tent. No, a teepee.

EMILE: From long sticks we found.

ALLA: *(Laughs.)* We pretended to be Indians.

EMILE: It was a secret place.

ALLA: No one would find us.

EMILE: Do you remember what we hid there?

ALLA: *(Nods her head.)* Yes. Broken pieces of… plates, cups. That people throw away.

EMILE: Blue and white. Shards. You could find them along the road.

ALLA: I took a whole one from my parents.

EMILE: *(Shakes his finger.)* You shouldn't have done that.

ALLA: We buried them.

EMILE: Treasures.

ALLA: The teepee fell down after you left. But the blue and white pieces are probably there, underground. *(She smiles.)* Come and look for them, Pan Emile.

END OF SCENE

SCENE 24

1992. Frieda older, in her room or 1943 attic. Time unimportant.

FRIEDA: Emile is always saying we should go back, visit Strody. Go back *(Bitter.)* To what? To look for bones? *(Covers her face with her hands. Long pause.)*

But I had a dream… that Emile and I did go back to Strody. Where Ukrainian girls in red and black embroidery sing a song, offer us bread and salt. *(Pause.)* For we are guests in their town, aren't we?

But we look down, May turns December, snow begins to fall, outline the scratches in the paving stones. So they grow into Hebrew letters. Faint letters. We have pictures of the cemetery after the war. The stones were still there. Now nothing.

We stand in a minefield. I can't move. I have trouble seeing in the snow.

END OF SCENE

SCENE 25

1992, next day. Pressner house. Entire family at dinner

HEATHER: What was she like, grandma?

FRIEDA: A nice lady, spoke good Polish too.

TAMAR: That's why I said hello, and left. Didn't mean to be unfriendly, I just thought you and Emile needed to be with her. And translating for me would have put a crimp in your conversation.

FRIEDA: She liked our poppy seed cake.

DANNY: *(Mouth full.)* Who wouldn't?

FRIEDA: The *(She pronounces the next word with relish.)* ingredients in America are better.

HEATHER: Oh, grandma, you're always like that. America is the best.

DANNY: I heard she brought a ring of yours.

EMILE: I told them the story, mammi. It was your wedding ring, wasn't it?

FRIEDA: I gave it back to her.

DANNY: Why did you do....

HEATHER: Why not keep it?

FRIEDA: Because. *(Pause.)*

EMILE: I can explain what grandma means.

TAMAR: Why not let her speak for herself?

EMILE: Tamar, please let's not get into that again. Because it's hard for her to say it.

HEATHER: Why wouldn't she take it? It was so nice of Mrs…. I can't remember her name.

EMILE: Because the ring was the Oleskos'. Grandma was saying "We had an agreement. We paid you, you hid us. You held to your part, we'll keep ours. That ring is yours."

DANNY: *(To Frieda.)* Is that what you meant, grandma?

FRIEDA: *(Long silence.)* We don't owe them anything.

HEATHER: You could have thanked her, grandma. For the offer of returning the ring. For saving you.

FRIEDA: My sister Roiza had nothing to thank them for. They waited till she was too weak to run, then gave her away. But took her money first.

EMILE: But Mammi, it wasn't the Oleskos who killed your sister.

FRIEDA: They're all the same.

EMILE: Please, mammi.

TAMAR: I wasn't there, Frieda. But they are not all the same. They are people, men and women. Each different. Some good, some bad. Some betrayed their Jewish friends. Some saved them.

DANNY: For money?

EMILE: Some for money.

TAMAR: Some because they had pity.

EMILE: Some because they were Communists.

TAMAR: Some because they were real Christians.

EMILE: Some because they knew the Russians would win the war.

TAMAR: Some for their friends.

FRIEDA: After the war, three young boys who survived, the Sobels from the next village, went back to their farm. To pick some things up, what was left over. They killed them. After the war. I can't forget my father. I can't forget my husband. My sister. The Sobel boys.

Lights Out
Spot on Emile and Tamar Downstage

TAMAR: Emile, are you afraid of upsetting your mother?

EMILE: She's been hurt enough. Why open those wounds?

TAMAR: Memories have a way of coming back, whether you like it or not. But you never fight with your mother. Even when she says outrageous things that I know you don't like. Like calling all Ukrainians murderers.

EMILE: I do set her straight, gently. You just heard me.

TAMAR: Gently. Maybe you're afraid she'll get angry at you.

EMILE: True, I don't like anger, directed toward me, or others… OK, it's cathartic. You let go, you don't keep it deep inside. But it's so damn destructive, Tamar. The Ukrainians, angry at the Soviets, take it out on the Jews. Who hate the Ukrainians, one and all. It never stops.

TAMAR: It must stop. But I'm talking about your mother and you.

EMILE: Why would I be afraid of her anger?

TAMAR: Because… part of you is still in the attic. There was love, wonderful love around you. Like a cocoon. Your mother, your uncle. And outside – terrible danger. You're worried still, now, that if your mother gets angry with you, you'd lose her love. And back there, in the attic, nothing, nothing would then protect you from the dark outside.

END OF SCENE

SCENE 26

1943 Attic. Young Emile, young Frieda.

EMILE: Tell me a story, Mammi.

FRIEDA: What would you like to hear?

EMILE: About the other Emile.

FRIEDA: The man you were named after, Emile Zola?

EMILE: Yes.

FRIEDA: I've told you his story a few times already. What I know of it.

EMILE: Please tell it again.

FRIEDA: He was a great writer in France.

EMILE: *(Eager.)* I know where France is, on the map.

FRIEDA: I know you do.

EMILE: Can we go there? *(He sees his mother hesitate.)* When the war is over?

FRIEDA: We will one day, Emile. Zola wrote novels that I and your father liked.

EMILE: What's a novel?

FRIEDA: It's a story. A long story, so that it takes up a whole book.

EMILE: Is it a true story? Like what you told me about the Norwegian explorer, Frid…

FRIEDA: Fridtjof Nansen. Who let his ship be frozen into the ice to drift with it across the North Pole.

EMILE: Stuck in the ice, brrr. The way we are here.

FRIEDA: Except he wanted to be there. Yes, that was a real story. But Zola's stories were made up. Maybe like the fairy tales I sometimes read for you. Like Robinson Crusoe.

EMILE: But what he wrote about Captain Dreyfus wasn't made up!

FRIEDA: *(Surprised.)* You remember that story!

EMILE: *(Proudly.)* I do. Captain Dreyfus was a great Jewish officer. The French army didn't like Jews. So they said he was a spy.

FRIEDA: They put him on Devil's Island. Emile Zola wrote…

EMILE: And broke his sword.

FRIEDA: You remember that.

EMILE: And ripped off his… *(Motions to shoulders.)*

FRIEDA: Epaulettes. That's what they are called.

EMILE: Did Captain Dreyfus have a gun?

FRIEDA: I don't know. But he was an army officer. I suppose he had one.

EMILE: Uncle Ernie has a gun.

FRIEDA: *(Amazed. Quietly, for Ernie is sleeping nearby.)* Emile, how do you know that?

EMILE: *(Smiling.)* I was a journalist, like Emile Zola. One night, I pretended to sleep. I saw Uncle Ernie cleaning it.

FRIEDA: You shouldn't have.

EMILE: And counting his bullets.

FRIEDA: Oh, my God!

EMILE: He has only eight. Mammi?

FRIEDA: Yes, Emile.

EMILE: Why does Uncle Ernie have a gun?

FRIEDA: To *(Thinks hard what to say.)* … protect us, if the Germans come.

EMILE: But they won't come in here, will they?

END OF SCENE

SCENE 27

1992, Pressner house, Frieda's room. Frieda jolts up in bed, to see Alla, who may be sitting in a chair or standing near Frieda's bed. There's a hint of ghostliness to Alla; maybe she is not really there.

ALLA: It is not easy to talk of those days.

FRIEDA: I live them each night.

ALLA: There is so much we don't know of your life, Pani Frieda.

FRIEDA: There's not much to tell, Pani Alla. You can see, we survived, we live well.

ALLA: But before. And after.

FRIEDA: Ask my son. But what do you mean "before"?

ALLA: Before you came to … our house.

FRIEDA: We were in a camp, which sometimes sent people to work in Gribniv. Your father and my Daniel talked. That's how we got to you.

ALLA: What did you do in the camp?

FRIEDA: Do? I cooked for 200 people, soup and things. And I ironed the lice. There was typhus.

ALLA: You had your son with you, in the camp?

FRIEDA: He was my life. How many times my husband said, let's leave him with some people, he'll survive. And we'll go into the forest. But I would not let go of my child. *(Pause.)* So I lost my husband instead.

ALLA: Pani Frieda, There's something my father didn't tell you. He had a brother, who died in 1941.

FRIEDA: He must have been young.

ALLA: Younger than my father.

FRIEDA: Was he sick?

ALLA: No, he was killed by the NKVD in the Strody castle. The Soviets took many of our educated people there, you know - he was a teacher too. They shot him in the last days of June 1941.

FRIEDA: And Daniel was shot in the last days of June 1943. Two terrible years for us. We died 50 times a day.

ALLA: It was a terrible time, worse for you, I know.

FRIEDA: Why are you telling me this, Alla? About your uncle. Some of your people are crazy enough to think we did that. As if we were the Soviets. As if we had guns.

ALLA: You didn't do it.

FRIEDA: You want sympathy?

ALLA: No, Pani Frieda. No sympathy needed. It happened. Those were terrible times. I just wanted to tell you... because my father wouldn't tell you.

FRIEDA: Why wouldn't he tell me?

ALLA: Because... he thought that if you knew how his brother died... that you wouldn't trust him. To hide you.

FRIEDA: *(Thinks.)* He was a good man.

END OF SCENE

SCENE 28

1992. Emile older. Time unimportant.

EMILE:
Two roses bloomed
in a Polish town.
In Hebrew they were
Shoshanah; one
they called Roza, one
Roiza. Both – Reyzele.
A brother of one
married a sister of the other.
Shoshanat Yaakov,
the rose of Jacob,
they were fragrant
to their parents;
if there were thorns,
no one now is left
to remember.

The war came.
One hot summer
Roza stood with her parents
for seven days
at our Strody station,
waiting for a transport
to take them to Belzec.
Her brother, my father,
passed, heard them
begging for water.
The guards raised their guns;
he had a wife and a child,

he went on.
They told them to strip,
looking for lice, they said;
Roza stood naked,
pink with shame
in the eyes of her father.

In Polish gardens
roses grew well
the last spring of the war.
The other rose,
Roiza and a friend
lay under a barn,
in mouldy blankets,
in their smell.
The Ukrainian who
owned the farm
for a while brought bread,
kielbasa, an old apple,
water. Then
he stopped,
they grew weak,
and one day,
when he knew they couldn't run,
he brought the police.

All flowers wilt, all bushes die.
But not this way, not a cut rose.

END OF SCENE

SCENE 29

1992, next day. Pressner house, Heather and Danny.

HEATHER: Why do you think she came to see grandma?

DANNY: To get something out of her.

HEATHER: How can you say that, Danny? She wanted to give grandma something, a ring!

DANNY: That was just a tactic. You know, like in a war. You pretend to be friends, lure the soldiers into the house, and... Pow!

HEATHER: You're crazy, too many video games in your head. What tactic?

DANNY: I'm crazy. OK, no ambush. But she wants something from us. They're having a hard time there, she comes here to work.

HEATHER: I don't blame her. Poor people.

DANNY: Listen. We send them packages, they know we feel we owe them something.

HEATHER: We do. Even you and me.

DANNY: Yeah. So they think: How can we get more out of those people?

HEATHER: That's awful. It's so... calculating.

DANNY: That's how they are. You've heard grandma talk.

HEATHER: No, they aren't. Not Alla. *(Pause.)* I could see it in her face.

DANNY: They see us as a source of money. Again.

HEATHER: No, no. I think about Alla and her husband sorting through her mother's things, finding that ring with grandma and grandpa's initials...

DANNY: Guessing it came from the Jewish family her parents hid.

HEATHER: Maybe it wasn't that obvious. Maybe her parents didn't talk much about the war. Just like grandma and pappa didn't tell us.

DANNY: Bah.

HEATHER: And in the Ukraine it was dangerous to talk about what happened in the war. They were under the Communists, their enemies. Pappa said that the teacher's students were in a Ukrainian, what did he call it...

DANNY: ... partisan group...

HEATHER: ...in the forest. Fighting the commies long after the war.

DANNY: And killing the Jews during the war. I can see a video game around that. Maybe it would have a good market in the Ukraine.

HEATHER: You're horrible.

DANNY: *(Makes a face at her.)*

HEATHER: I don't think Alla sat down and said "Those were terrible times for the Jews. We have to make up for it." I think she was just reaching out, for something that we had in common.

DANNY: So we would owe them.

HEATHER: No. They had something that had been ours. That then was their parents. Then theirs. That could be ours again. *(Pause.)* They weren't scheming. People are not like that.

DANNY: You don't want them to be that way, you mean.

HEATHER: I don't want to be that way.

END OF SCENE

SCENE 30

1992, Emile older, alone, anywhere on stage

EMILE: Now I had a dream. It was in one of the concentration camps, the ones we didn't get into:

On the day the guards ran, before the Russians marched in and the shelling grew louder, a man emptied the barrack slop pail and went looking for blood. He found men, clumsy at butchering a cow. They pushed him off, but when he said it was only blood he wanted, they let him catch it, spurting from the neck. The man lifted a board, took out his clay figures. *(He stops, for moment, worrying the audience will not understand him.)*

Do you know the story of the Golem? How you make one? *(Pause, decides to go on.)*

He set them in a circle in the dirt, a woman and child in the middle, then walked around, his hand dipping to the elbow in the bucket, throwing blood at the feet of the clay people.

And when they didn't move, the man called their names, one by one, and sang the *Shma*[4] backwards, and desperate, smeared more blood on their poorly formed faces, knocking them over, and in the end, cursed God hoarsely in both Yiddish and Romanian.

END OF SCENE

SCENE 31

1992, next day, Pressner house, Emile and Tamar.

(We enter in the middle of a heated discussion.)

TAMAR: *(Hands on ears.)* Stop, you have to stop calling them "The Ukrainians," "The Germans!"

EMILE: Why? They called us the Jews. They killed us for that.

TAMAR: Some Germans, Some Ukrainians killed you.

EMILE: Many Germans, Many Ukrainians. Warzok the beast, as my mother calls him. The SS men at the castle, and the ones who liquidated the ghetto. Not one, ten, twenty, a hundred. Thousands.

TAMAR: What about Olesko, who made the hard decision to hide you, with his small children in the house?

EMILE: For everyone like him there were dozens who killed and robbed and betrayed. It's you who reminded me of that. Where are their stories, you said.

TAMAR: You have to say "This man, Olesko, a Ukrainian hid us." "This SS man, Warzok, a sadist, a Nazi, killed dozens of Jews."

EMILE: And the country, the society, that… allowed their cruelty, that encouraged it, that made it part of their duty?

TAMAR: Blame the society, blame the culture. But leave the men and women who chose… evil, leave them as individuals. Who, in a terrible time, chose to hurt others. When they could have helped with a crust of bread.

EMILE: And how many cruel men — for they were mostly men — how many inhuman German men do you need before you can say "The Germans did it?"

TAMAR: It's not a logic of this world…

EMILE: There is no other world. My father was killed in this world.

TAMAR: *(Takes a breath in and out.)* I would say that as long as there is one good man, one good woman who is German… you cannot say it, you can't say "The Germans…"

EMILE: A weird logic, where one trumps many.

TAMAR: One good man redeems the world.

EMILE: Sounds Christian.

TAMAR: It's also Jewish. *(Pause.)* A strange logic, not very scientific. But we couldn't live on without it.

END OF SCENE

SCENE 32

1992, Emile, Frieda, perhaps in kitchen.

EMILE: Mammi, I meant to ask you. I have this memory of someone else in the attic with us.

FRIEDA: Who? There was Uncle Ernie, you, I.

EMILE: A little girl.

FRIEDA: A little girl.

EMILE: Was I dreaming?

FRIEDA: I wish you were. *(Sighs.)* I wish you were, Emile. You were not dreaming. In the beginning there was a little girl with us.

EMILE: What do you mean 'in the beginning'?

FRIEDA: When we went in the attic. Sabina.

EMILE: So I wasn't dreaming.

FRIEDA: Ernie's Sabina.

EMILE: His daughter.

FRIEDA: Yes, his daughter. Her mother, they killed in the first week. He had his daughter…

EMILE: What happened to her?

FRIEDA: You don't remember?

EMILE: No. *(Pause.)* Yes. Sometimes she slept next to me. We whispered to each other. But what happened to her?

FRIEDA: She cried.

EMILE: I cried.

FRIEDA: You, I could stop. I'd give you a book. *(Pause.)* But Sabina *(Pause)* just cried.

EMILE: How old was she?

FRIEDA: Two, or three. Two when we went in. She cried and she cried. We decided she couldn't keep quiet. So Uncle Ernie went out at night, found a Polish family who would take her, gave them money…

EMILE: *(Looks at her)*…

FRIEDA: A month she cried. There were people in the house – Olesko was nervous.

EMILE: So you gave Sabina away?

FRIEDA: Don't say it that way. We had to do it. We had to. We gave her away to save her.

EMILE: *(Quiet.)* She's not alive. Uncle Ernie doesn't have a daughter,

FRIEDA: After the war, Ernie went to the village. They said the Germans killed the Polish family. Or maybe it was the Ukrainians who killed her – anyway someone else was living in their house. And no one knew where the child was.

EMILE: She's dead, because she cried.

FRIEDA: *(Nods.)* And you didn't.

EMILE: You haven't told me this before.

FRIEDA: *(Shrugs. Then thinks)* Don't tell the kids. I don't want them to know God gives us such choices.

END OF SCENE

SCENE 33

1992, next day. Pressner house kitchen: Emile, Tamar, Danny, Heather. Frieda is listening, the others do not see her.

HEATHER: I read about these courts in Africa. Where people who took part in killings are tried by their neighbors.

DANNY: That won't work here.

HEATHER: Why not? The killers say they did it, ask to be forgiven.

EMILE: And it's too late, Heather, much too late. For 45 years after the war the Communists ran the Ukraine. In the Soviets' perverted view of history, Jews were killed by the Nazis not because they were Jews, but because they were Russians, or Poles. For 45 years the Soviets didn't let the Ukrainians think about their part in the killing.

DANNY: And now? When they are free? Do they think about it?

EMILE: You remember that castle above Strody? Where my grandfather was killed? *(Growing angrier, sarcastic.)* No pogrom brought the Jews to that castle, they now say. No Ukrainian part in it. And if the SS killed some Jews, well, it was outside the walls of the castle. *(Pause.)* Inside, no – a pretty garden now over the killing ground, must have been a garden then. They just want a tourist attraction there..

(Silent moment.)

TAMAR: You know, a little forgetting is not a bad thing. It has a role in getting people past trauma.

HEATHER: Mom, how could you let the Ukrainians forget?

TAMAR: I'm not talking about the Ukrainians. The killers among them… to them forgetting comes all too naturally. Along with rationalization: "We beat them because they robbed our fathers." "There were Jews in the NKVD." Freud rest in peace, for the killers little will surface. *(Pause.)* Their young people, they're the ones who need to remember.
(Sighs. Slowly) I was thinking about the survivors, the ones with nightmares. That they would *(Pause.)* will to forget. At least a little.

DANNY: How can they forget if they see the murderers go free? You need justice.

TAMAR: But after justice, when you're still unable to forgive? Forgetting is the part of forgiving no one talks about, because forgiving is good, forgetting is… a weakness.

EMILE: This is weird, Tamar. You're a psychologist. All the time you try to take your clients back to their childhood. You help them remember. Now you want them to forget?

TAMAR: I know. But I still think it's a piece of what has to happen. You need to remember enough so you allow yourself to come out of hiding. To mourn. *(Pause.)* And, yes, a country needs to remember, so that it won't happen again. so that our children never / have to experience…

EMILE: *(Interrupts.)* And then a politician comes along, calls up those hundred year old injustices against the people! Like the Serbs did in Bosnia.

TAMAR: I hate them, Emile, as much as you do — they pretend to remember, only to get others to kill.
(Silence for a moment.)

HEATHER: I think it's OK for grandma to hate. *(Pause.)* I don't like myself for saying it.

DANNY: She's been so hurt.

TAMAR: If she could meet a Ukrainian woman who suffered like her. If they could cry together, for each other. If…

EMILE: Too many ifs, Tamar. My mother's world can't be put together again.

TAMAR: You're right. The dead weigh on her *(Pause.)* She can't admit there were others like the Oleskos; she thanks them only with packages. *(With rising intensity.)* But listen to her stories. Listen. She tells of the nun she loved in that convent in Vienna. She tells the story of the Ukrainian nanny in World War I. She's looking for the good. Still. Despite what the war did to her. *(Pause.)* I worry more about you.

END OF SCENE

SCENE 34

1992 older Emile, in attic.

EMILE: Others had come back
long after the war was over,
so I was sure you had not died, father.
As they marched you through town,
probably you just broke free, ran.
They'd shot another in your place. One day
you would come, gaunt, threadbare,
to tell stories from the marshes where you hid.
One day you'd come back,
walking the long road from Russia.

And when you failed me
and didn't come,
I asked my mother
to tell me one more time
what had happened,
and I willed myself into the mind
of the Jew who informed on you,
oh my father,
who gave away your hidden guns,
your break-out plans.
I told him how brave you were.

When this didn't work, father,
I dreamed I had powers,
that I could pump vodka into the blood,
slow the Ukrainian policeman
who pulled his gun when you lunged at the
SS trooper.

And when this too failed, oh father,
I closed the shutters
and turned away the faces
of the people forced to watch in the square,
so they would not see you fall,
so they need not hear you say,
twice, my mother's name.

END OF SCENE

SCENE 35

1992, Emile and Tamar, downstage. Time indeterminate.

TAMAR: Alla brought you something else than Frieda's ring. Something… that you can't ask her to take back.

EMILE: What?

TAMAR: Memory, memories.

EMILE: They weren't Alla's to give. I have them. Mammi has them. They're ours.

TAMAR: But they were buried in you.

EMILE: Oh, I know. I was the one who buried them. OK. She comes here, the memories surface. And Mammi has nightmares. What's good about that?

TAMAR: *(Emotion rising.)* Look, Emile, let me be selfish. Until we found out that Alla was coming, Heather, Danny and I knew damn little about what happened to your mother and you during the war. "A Ukrainian hid us out. In an attic," you said, "My husband died in an attempt to break out of the camp," she said. We felt that you didn't want to talk about the war, and we knew that it hurt. So we didn't push you, and certainly not Frieda.

But how many times did the children ask me, did I know where you were hidden? Why wasn't your father with you? Or kid stuff: How did you go to the toilet up in the attic? They asked me. And I couldn't tell them a thing.

Now Alla comes, and you talk. And your mother finally answers Heather's questions.

EMILE: But it can't be that Alla knew that this would happen, that she... intended to give us back those memories.

TAMAR: Of course not! I try to imagine what she thought when she first saw that ring, and realized that it couldn't be her mother's. How she linked it with the little her parents told her about us. She made the connection, thought that once it was something of ours. And that it would be right, and good to give it back. A simple gift, a ring.

EMILE: A simple gift it wasn't. I like her, she meant well. But she opened something that should have stayed closed.

TAMAR: What do you mean? What did she open?

EMILE: An agreement. Sealed when Frieda and her brother paid Olesko. In '43 and '44. Alla cut it open again. By returning the ring.

TAMAR: No, No. That seal is just a cover for not wanting to think about those times. Emile, listen to me. The tie between Frieda, Ernie, you, between our family and Alla's family, coming out of those terrible times of the war, is just there. Forever.

EMILE: *(Thinks.)* You're right. *(Pause.)* It just hurts so much to think about ... what happened. Again. *(Close to breaking up.)* About my father. After all those years.

TAMAR: I know it hurts. *(Gently.)* Alla was …crafting a new link between us, gently, with no designs, with… love, reaching into the past for her materials. *(Pause.)* Can you see that?

EMILE: *(Pause.)* I think I can. *(Pause.)* In a way *(beat)* we did that too, sending packages to Gribniv all those years.

TAMAR: Yes, it wasn't that Frieda and Ernie felt guilty, that they hadn't paid the Oleskos enough during the war.

EMILE: It was a hand stretched out.

TAMAR: Showing that you still cared. And remembered. As you do today.

END OF SCENE

SCENE 36

Attic. 1943-1992 mixed. Emile, Frieda

FRIEDA: Every day we looked death in the eye.

EMILE: *(Gestures to her.)* She's proud of her English. Were you scared, mammi?

FRIEDA: Yes. *(Then she smiles, the rare smile of the sick.)* *(Pause.)* Death looked away.

EMILE: *(To audience.)* I was there. But a child can't see. I imagine now my mother, her brother, and me in the attic, in our long dark evenings *(Beat.)* for what if Olesko's neighbors saw a light?
(The following, to end, is read as a poem, with pauses as appropriate.)
There, listen, death comes riding, into small village noises, Death, with spats, holster, a whip, breaking branches as he rides. Working his way through lists, ridding green earth of a worm.

FRIEDA: In the eye.

EMILE: His roaming stops, by Olesko's school. Inside, they hear hoofbeats, that halt. Death spots them, across two walls. And they look him in the eye. But then Death, boots, spurs and all, smells stale cabbage soup, which reminds him of the dying, soiling themselves. He looks away, fastidious death.

FRIEDA: And comes back the next day.

END OF SCENE

SCENE 37

1992, Pressner house, time indeterminate Emile and Frieda.

EMILE: What do you want, mammi?

FRIEDA: Justice.

EMILE: Justice? And what does that mean?

FRIEDA: What they deserve.

EMILE: Which is what?

FRIEDA: *(Says nothing.)*

EMILE: That they would die?

FRIEDA: Yes.

EMILE: All of them? Even Olesko?

FRIEDA: *(Grudgingly.)* Most of them.

EMILE: But that wouldn't bring pappa back. Or your sister. It won't make a new world, where this couldn't happen again.

FRIEDA: But they would know what we went through. Our children living in mouseholes. Our women...

EMILE: You know, mammi, they've lived their own hell, to be under the Communists, their worst enemy.

FRIEDA: They earned it.

EMILE: You hate them.

FRIEDA: I hate them. *(Pause.)* Don't I have reasons to? *(Both are quiet.)*

EMILE: And you think I don't hate enough.

FRIEDA: For me you don't hate enough. For you, it's right.

EMILE: I don't understand, mammi.

FRIEDA: I can't explain it.

EMILE: Try.

FRIEDA: *(Long Pause.)* In the attic, where you couldn't stand up, what do you remember, Emile?

EMILE: Little, mammi. I should remember more. Maybe there was a reason to forget. *(Pause, as he tries to remember.)* Peas in the pillow, the window. Geography books. Uncle Ernie coming in sick. His gun, that you didn't want me to see. Reading by the window. A smell. *(Pause.)* You, lying next to you.

FRIEDA: Do you remember what we talked about?

EMILE: Everything, mammi. The games you made up. My father, how he built roads. Ships and railroads. What Vienna was like, when you studied there. The kids in Africa in that book.

FRIEDA: Did I teach you to hate? In that mousehole, where every day lasted forever, did I teach a child to hate?

END OF SCENE

SCENE 38

1992. Entire house, attic included. Cast spread through house or stage. If separate actors are used for younger Emile and Frieda, they are there too. Spot on Frieda first, remains on her. A second, brighter spot then picks up the others in turn. There is a flame on stage, a real one or a projection. Alla, who doesn't speak in this scene, tends to the flame throughout the scene.

FRIEDA: I had a dream, children. *(Pause.)* But I'm old, *(Beat.)* and I forget the dreams too. *(She muses.)* A strange one, full of gold. And not a nightmare…
(She looks toward the fire. During the scene, Frieda moves all the time, while the others freeze when they do not speak.)

TAMAR: *(Picks up or holds the golden boxes. Or one of them.)*
A large room was built
for the ceremony; we
enter, to forget, put an
end to, forget. Each
brings a golden box,
you do, and I. Some carry
two or three. In each box
a scroll, a memory
written in Serbian, or
Yiddish, in Armenian,
Turkish, Chinese, Hutu,
Croatian, and Ukrainian.
For this we prepared
a year, writing each day
until no more could be

91

written, writing more
the next day. We stack
the boxes in the center
of the room, where fire
comes; we sit and watch
them burn, burn all night.
All around the world,
for six days, people burn
the gilt boxes of forgetting.

*(As her lines draw to a close, she takes her box — or the
script in a reading – and determinedly throws it in the fire.)*

DANNY:
Last year we were
on Mauna Kea, on
the big island
of Hawaii, there
the lava flows
have neat brown
signs. Pele's
'89 act still

HEATHER:
has whiffs of sulfur
dioxide; '86's
black cinders
cut my shoes,
but after ten years,
there are flowers,
in fifty
good earth.

(As Heather's lines draw to a close, she and Danny both do as Tamar did, but with their own inflection on the action.)

EMILE: *(Emile begins with the intention of following the others, moving to the fire. Then he hesitates in anguish, turns to his mother, speaks.)*
Forty-nine years ago
they killed you, father.
How shall I fill
my golden box
of forgetting, when
I could not, at five,
nestle in your arms?

(As the play ends, Emile turns his back to the fire and grips the golden box –or his script – close to his chest.)

LIGHTS OUT (except on flame)

END OF SCENE AND ACT 2
END OF PLAY

NOTES

1) A designation by *Yad vaShem*, the Israeli Holocaust Remembrance organization, of those non-Jews who courageously helped Jews during World War II.

2) This is a Polish children's classic by Henryk Sienkiewicz. Every Polish child read it. Staś and Nell are the protagonists – a Polish boy and an English girl.

3) Poppy seed cake

4) Jewish Creed: *Shma Yisrael, Adonai...*, part of the formula for creating a Golem

The first production of "Something That Belongs to You" was a staged reading at the University of Richmond, Richmond, Va. Sept. 14, 15, 16 2009.

Director...................... Walter Schoen
Stage Manager............... Donna E. Coghill
Producer..................... Paul Kappel

Cast

Frieda........................... Dorothy Holland
Emile............................ Rusty Wilson
Alla............................. Irene Ziegler
Tamar.......................... Julie Fulcher
Heather......................... GlennMary Carroll
Danny........................... Patrick Jones

The first full performance of the play was in German (transl. Hartmut Frank), as *Was Euch Gehört*, Bayreuth, Germany, StadtHalle, Kleines Haus, Sept. 27, 2014.

Jan Burdinski

Director.................... Karin Pollak
Scenery....................

Cast Marsha Cox

Frieda...................... Markus Veith
Emil....................... Laura Mann
Tamar...................... Bettina Wagner
Heather.................... Alexander Boock
Danny......................Carolin Barczyk
Alla........................ Kirsten Annika Lange
Young Frieda.............. Lars Eichhorn
Young Emil.................

ABOUT THE AUTHOR

ROALD HOFFMANN was born in 1937 in Złoczów, then Poland. He came to the US in 1949, and has long been at Cornell University, active as a theoretical chemist. In chemistry he has taught his colleagues how to think about electrons influencing structure and reactivity, and won most of the honors of his profession.

Hoffmann is also a writer, carving out his own land between poetry, philosophy, and science. He has published five books of non-fiction, and six volumes of poetry, including two book length selections of his poems in Spanish and Russian translations. This is his third play (all of which have been produced); the others are "Oxygen", with Carl Djerassi, and "Should've."

Books by Dos Madres Press

Mary Margaret Alvarado - Hey Folly (2013)

John Anson - Jose-Maria de Heredia's Les Trophées (2013),
    Time Pieces - poems & translations (2014)

Jennifer Arin - Ways We Hold (2012)

Michael Autrey - From The Genre Of Silence (2008)

Stuart Bartow - Einstein's Lawn (2015)

Paul Bray - Things Past and Things to Come (2006), Terrible Woods (2008)

Ann Cefola - Face Painting in the Dark (2014)

Jon Curley - New Shadows (2009), Angles of Incidents (2012)

Grace Curtis - The Shape of a Box (2014)

Sara Dailey - Earlier Lives (2012)

Dennis Daly - Nightwalking with Nathaniel-poems of Salem (2014)

Richard Darabaner - Plaint (2012)

Deborah Diemont - Wanderer (2009), Diverting Angels (2012)

Joseph Donahue - The Copper Scroll (2007)

Annie Finch - Home Birth (2004)

Norman Finkelstein - An Assembly (2004), Scribe (2009)

Karen George - Swim Your Way Back (2014)

Gerry Grubbs - Still Life (2005), Girls in Bright Dresses Dancing (2010),
    The Hive-a book we read for its honey (2013)

Richard Hague - Burst, Poems Quickly (2004),
    During The Recent Extinctions (2012), Where Drunk Men Go (2015)

Ruth D. Handel - Tugboat Warrior (2013), No Border is Perennial (2015)

Pauletta Hansel - First Person (2007), What I Did There (2011), Tangle (2015)

Michael Heller - A Look at the Door with the Hinges Off (2006),
    Earth and Cave (2006)

Michael Henson - The Tao of Longing & The Body Geographic (2010)

R. Nemo Hill - When Men Bow Down (2012)

W. Nick Hill - And We'd Understand Crows Laughing (2012)

Eric Hoffman - Life At Braintree (2008), The American Eye (2011),
    By the Hours (2013), Forms of Life (2015)

Roald Hoffmann - Something That BelongsTo You (2015)

James Hogan - Rue St. Jacques (2005)

Keith Holyoak - My Minotaur (2010), Foreigner (2012),
    The Gospel According to Judas (2015)

Nancy Kassell - Text(isles) (2013)

David M. Katz - Claims of Home (2011), Stanzas on Oz (2015)

Sherry Kearns - Deep Kiss (2013), The Magnificence of Ruin (2015)

Marjorie Deiter Keyishian - Ashes and All (2015)

Burt Kimmelman - There Are Words (2007), The Way We Live (2011)

Jill Kelly Koren - The Work of the Body (2015)

Ralph La Charity - Farewellia a la Aralee (2014)

Pamela L. Laskin - Plagiarist (2012)

Owen Lewis - Sometimes Full of Daylight (2013), Best Man (2015)

Richard Luftig - Off The Map (2006)

Austin MacRae - The Organ Builder (2012)

Mario Markus - Chemical Poems-One For Each Element (2013)

J. Morris - The Musician, Approaching Sleep (2006)

Patricia Monaghan - Mary-A Life in Verse (2014)

Rick Mullin - Soutine (2012), Coelacanth (2013),
    Sonnets on the Voyage of the Beagle (2014)

Fred Muratori - A Civilization (2014)

Robert Murphy - Not For You Alone (2004), Life in the Ordovician (2007),
    From Behind The Blind (2013)

Pam O'Brien - The Answer To Each Is The Same (2012)

Peter O'Leary - A Mystical Theology of the Limbic Fissure (2005)

Bea Opengart - In The Land (2011)

David A. Petreman - Candlelight in Quintero-bilingual ed. (2011)

Paul Pines - Reflections in a Smoking Mirror (2011),
    New Orleans Variations & Paris Ouroboros (2013),
    Fishing on the Pole Star (2014)
    Message from the Memoirist (2015)

Quanita Roberson - Soul Growing-Wisdom for thirteen year old boys from
    men around the world (2015)

William Schickel - What A Woman (2007)

Don Schofield - In Lands Imagination Favors (2014)

David Schloss - Behind the Eyes (2005), Reports from Babylon and Beyond (2015)

Daniel Shapiro - The Red Handkerchief and other poems (2014)

Murray Shugars - Songs My Mother Never Taught Me (2011),
Snakebit Kudzu (2013)

Jason Shulman - What does reward bring you but to bind you to
Heaven like a slave? (2013)

Maxine Silverman - Palimpsest (2014)

Lianne Spidel & Anne Loveland - Pairings (2012), A Bird in the Hand (2014)

Olivia Stiffler - Otherwise, we are safe (2013)

Carole Stone - Hurt, the Shadow-the Josephine Hopper poems (2013)

Nathan Swartzendruber - Opaque Projectionist (2009)

Jean Syed - Sonnets (2009)

Eileen R. Tabios - INVENT[ST]ORY Selected Catalog Poems and New 1996-
2015 (2015)

Madeline Tiger - The Atheist's Prayer (2010), From the Viewing Stand (2011)

James Tolan - Red Walls (2011)

Brian Volck - Flesh Becomes Word (2013)

Henry Weinfield - The Tears of the Muses (2005), Without Mythologies (2008),
A Wandering Aramaean (2012)

Donald Wellman - A North Atlantic Wall (2010),
The Cranberry Island Series (2012)

Sarah White - The Unknowing Muse (2014)

Anne Whitehouse - The Refrain (2012)

Martin Willetts Jr. - Secrets No One Must Talk About (2011)

Tyrone Williams - Futures, Elections (2004), Adventures of Pi (2011)

Kip Zegers - The Poet of Schools (2013)

www.dosmadres.com